house beautiful

CHRISTMAS

house beautiful

CHRISTMAS

The Editors of House Beautiful Magazine

Louis Oliver Gropp, Editor in Chief • Margaret Kennedy, Editor

Text by Sally Clark

THE HEARST CORPORATION

NEW YORK

Library of Congress Cataloging-in-Publication Data

House Beautiful.
    House Beautiful Christmas / the editors of House Beautiful magazine; text by Sally Clark.
        p.   cm.
    Includes index.
    ISBN 0-688-12590-5
    1. Christmas—United States. 2. Christmas decorations—United States. 3. United States—Social life and customs.
I. House beautiful. II. Title.
GT4986.A1C53   1994
394.2'663—dc20   94-199
                                                                   CIP

Printed in Italy

First Edition

1 2 3 4 5 6 7 8 9 10

EDITED BY LAURIE ORSECK
DESIGNED BY NANCY STEINY
PRODUCED BY SMALLWOOD & STEWART, INC., NEW YORK

CONTENTS

FOREWORD

*C*hristmas is a holiday with rich religious meaning; it is no wonder that the traditions surrounding this day have taken on a life of their own. But the domestic side of Christmas has magic of its own, too, composed of three essential parts. The first is decorating ~ from the traditional vocabulary of red and green to fresh variations not immediately associated with the season. The second is celebrating. After years of Christmas festivities at home and at *House Beautiful,* I've learned that the tree gets star billing, collecting family memories as surely as it collects ornaments on its branches. And some delightful and surprising new ideas for wrapping gifts make both the giving and receiving more fun.

The third element is entertaining. Though family gatherings are such a special part of this season, most of us like to reach out to friends and neighbors as well. Feeling no one should be alone on Christmas Eve, a brother and sister we know always give a Christmas Eve party, with the guest list depending on who is without a family that year. A great idea, we think: Christmas is, after all, a time for sharing, and when that undergirds all the decorations, the celebrations, and the entertaining, the spirit of Christmas is present as well.

LOUIS OLIVER GROPP
EDITOR IN CHIEF

house beautiful

CHRISTMAS

INTRODUCTION

*C*hristmas is the most magical of celebrations. The holiday transforms a period of short days and chill weather into a time of warmth, generosity, and renewal. We dress up our homes to please ourselves and to welcome friends and family; we seek out gifts, carefully chosen and joyfully bestowed. Treasured ornaments are again brought out to hang on the tree. The old carols are sung once more. And everyone's favorite holiday meal is served on a splendidly set table. In all these ways, we renew our ties with our own families and in so doing return to our roots for these wonderful days.

But keeping the holiday vital often means creating new traditions as well as invoking old ones ~ maybe something as simple as filling the house with all-white ornaments and flowers rather than the usual reds and greens, or letting each child decorate his own Christmas tree. *House Beautiful Christmas* is a wonderful source of ideas for both approaches. The book is divided into three parts. The first, "Decorating," is rich in ideas for transforming the house with orna-

mentation as natural as lush green garlands or as elaborate as tabletops glittering with gold and silver baubles, and everything in the way of wreaths, topiaries, mantel arrangements, and festoons for doors, windows, and walls.

"Celebrating" addresses the more personal and perhaps spiritual traditions of the season, starting with the tree, the most cherished of all. There are dozens of alluring examples, from firs adorned with gauze bows to soaring evergreens decked out with ornaments as thin as a butterfly's wing.

"Entertaining" offers myriad possibilities for table settings and party feasts, whether casual buffet or formal sit-down dinner. The notions here are especially inventive ~ tablecloths fashioned from gold-embroidered saris, easy-to-create centerpieces, clever serving ideas using treasured collectibles.

We hope the ideas captured in *House Beautiful Christmas* will enrich your next holiday. By adapting the look of a wreath, the design of a table setting, or the mood of a fantasy room, you may just launch some wonderful new holiday traditions of your own.

DECORATING

Often it's the simplest design that makes the most charming Christmas decoration ~ consider, for example, unadorned evergreen ropes laid across the mantelpiece and twined around the banister. The emerald hues of nature are luxurious in their own right and need no embellishment. And the gathering of greens ~ whether a garland of feathery prince's pine from the local nursery or a homemade wreath ornamented with pinecones gathered from the garden ~ truly marks the start of the holiday season.

Of course, nature provides other possibilities for beautifying evergreens. Carolyn Gregg, a New York City garden expert, sets off juniper branches with ornaments made by stringing slices of dried fruit like beads on a

necklace. Florists Jack Follmer, Jr., and Spruce Roden surround a bubbly bouquet of pepper berries with the pinecone basket pictured on page 16. The pinecones are cut lengthwise, then glued to a plain container.

Certainly, nature can be glossed over, perhaps with strips of gold lace glued to a pomander ball or gilded ribbons trailing pine boughs on a mantel. Sometimes the holiday is a fine excuse to turn a room into a fantasy setting awash in gold, silver, and glitter. For John Saladino the decorations can never be too theatrical or glamorous. One year he draped his dining room tables in silver Mylar, "so they resemble ice skating rinks." Then he added amusing silver embellishments, laying ropes of glass beads at the table's center and scattering silver-colored dragées, usually reserved for decorating cookies.

Whether the sparkle of glass beads or the shine of silvery Mylar, these glittering decorations bring indoors the sheen of frost-laced December ~ and some of the magic of childhood Christmas memories.

*W*onderfully exuberant, David Madison's five-point star begins with a simple wooden base. Madison uses glue and wire to secure an abundance of dried natural ingredients, including wild grasses, herbs, mushrooms, and as a centerpiece, a beautifully preserved hydrangea (opposite).

Bill Crinnigan's enchanting topiary blossoms with fragrant whole lemons, kumquats, and orange slices (above). He built the miniature tree on a spiral wire form, applied moss with a glue gun, and secured the fruit with florist's wire.

$\mathcal{F}$or a few weeks rooms that are so familiar become utterly transformed as wreaths go up and garlands are hung around doorways and swagged on walls. These wreaths and garlands may be simple in design, just plain circles of pine and ropes of laurel. But the effect is rich and lush looking, turning a room into a forest–like bower fragrant with the leafy aroma and evergreen palette of the outdoors. How welcome the woodland's treasures are at a time of year when the days have grown short and the biting chill of winter hovers in the air.

Bringing holly, ivy, mistletoe, and pine into the house during the holidays is a tradition that Christmas borrowed from much older

$\mathcal{A}$ moss reindeer with whimsical twig antlers stands vigil over pots of perfumed hyacinth and brilliant red amaryllis blossoms (opposite). In the background, the photograph of a *putto* statue provides a charming seasonal image.

New York floral designer Zezé also likes to work with moss and twigs for his holiday decorations (left). Fresh green moss covers a tree-shaped frame, which is then wrapped with pliant twigs and topped with a gilt-edged ribbon. The ribbon has thin wire woven into it, so that it can be molded into virtually any shape.

celebrations that reach back to pre-Christian history. During the prolonged festivities of December and January honoring various gods, the Romans decked their houses with evergreens. Farther north, among Germanic peoples, sprays of greens were probably carried indoors as part of their midwinter feasts. The tree-worshipping Druids also ignited Yule logs cut from oak trees.

Working with natural greens gathered from garden and woodland, the Victorians created imaginative, lush ornaments that can inspire us today. Popular magazines offered instructions for inventive decorations crafted of greenery, such as a whimsical Christmas harp and lyre, their frames covered in leaves and the strings made of berries threaded on wire. Rooms were transformed into seasonal groves, with ropes of greens crisscrossing ceilings and looped into bosky valances. An enchanting portfolio of pen and ink drawings by Miss Lucy Ellen McErrill shows that in the fashionable New England room of the 1870s greenery was hung lavishly to follow the lines of the architecture. The rooms are evergreen fairylands, with ropes of greens tracing chair rails, swagged on dadoes, and cascading down doorways.

Natural materials appeal to us now, too, and particularly to floral artist Paul Bott, who chooses evergreens with an eye to texture and form. "Decorations are an extension of our own tastes and fantasy," he says. Blue spruce, blue atlas cedar, black pine, hemlock, and giant sugar pine laden with their huge cones are some of his favorite Christmas evergreens.

*M*ore than a dozen types of evergreens can be found in the richly textured, brilliant green wreaths that horticulturalist Allen C. Haskell uses to decorate the historic Rotch-Jones-Duff House in New Bedford, Massachusetts for Christmas (above).

Architects William McDonough and Elizabeth Demetriades piled up gifts wrapped in craft paper and tucked into recycled berry boxes (opposite).

*T*o light the way: A candle propped in a moss-banked clay pot is a simple decoration that becomes dramatic when several pots parade up a stairway (opposite). Designer Laura Bohn chose old pots with weathered surfaces that work well with the gunmetal-gray painted stairs. On the second-floor landing of an 1850 farmhouse, William McDonough and Elizabeth Demetriades placed a basket containing a small tree on an old rocking chair (above). On the floor, a stack of twig baskets waits to be wrapped with greenery.

*S*tems of greens, densely packed in a Styrofoam-filled florist's vase, are slipped into an ornamental container (above). Arranged with small objects such as the frame and beach stones here, the greens make an arresting holiday vignette.

A colorful bouquet of summer flowers marries beautifully with an urn studded with wintery pinecones (opposite). Floral Designers Jack Follmer, Jr., and Spruce Roden recommend large blue spruce cones for the base and smaller hemlock or alder cones for the arms. A collar of unshelled almonds completes the unusual look.

ℕatural ornaments aren't always green. Vivid orange and yellow citrus fruits can fill a room with sunshine (above). Whole cloves are pressed into the skins in a variety of designs; besides lemons and oranges, tangerines, clementines, and kumquats are good for pomanders. Garden writer Elvin McDonald decorated his evergreen wreaths with the promise of spring in the form of ready-to-plant narcissus bulbs (opposite). The bulbs are held in place with green string.

Christmas at Abbie Zabar's New York apartment means carefully edited decorations, sparely arranged. At the hearth in her contemporary, all-white apartment, she arranges natural fruits and greens to please her mood. Some days she selects furry cuttings of evergreens and whole apples or pears, and illuminates the arrangements with flickering votive candles (above left). Other times, the coppery surfaces and swelling shapes of succulent pears lining the mantel are decoration enough (below left).

A wealth of red berries was combined in the merry garnish of an eighteenth-century mantel. Bittersweet runners clipped in the woods were wound into a scarlet wreath, and in a vintage white pitcher are branches cut from a Jerusalem cherry bush purchased at a garden center. Brightening the cascade of greenery and handknitted stockings hung from the mantelpiece are strands of cranberries and nuggets of red peppercorns.

*T*he luscious little topiary of lady apples growing from a French wire basket was fashioned by New York floral artist Ronaldo Maia (above). Using a glue gun, he covered a Styrofoam ball with moss, then wedged it into a metal liner inserted in the basket. The apples were speared together with wooden toothpicks and sprayed with clear acrylic to preserve them for weeks.

A vintage kitchen container such as a patinated tin muffin tray, ramekin, or antique cutlery box (opposite) makes an ideal candleholder. Chunky candles in the box illuminate delicate vines arranged in an artful tangle. Watching over the scene from an antique portrait is a young girl in a ruby-red dress.

ECHOES OF CHRISTMASES PAST

The recipe for decorating his 1750 farmhouse was carefully worked out by David Webster weeks before December: a dash of nostalgia and a pinch of Scandinavia; handmade Victorian ornaments for the tree, and natural greenery for the rooms. The result: an enchanting setting for celebrating an old-fashioned country Christmas. For Webster, an interior designer, and his partner, Michael Erikson, mixing a few Christmas traditions seemed appropriate in a house that had undergone several stylistic changes over two centuries. When Webster bought the abandoned farmhouse in New York State, he identified Victorian embellishments and Greek Revival elements on top of the original colonial architecture. Peeling back layers, his investigations uncovered superb early features that had been concealed, including a huge stone cooking fireplace and wideboard floors. Webster painted the restored walls milky white and the trim in radiant colonial hues ~ evergreen in the master bedroom, yellow ocher in the living room, and velvety taupe and red in the kitchen. Those rich colors are enhanced by the natural greens he hangs in every room at Christmas.

The idea of using natural greens in a Scandinavian fashion was proposed by the late James E. Goslee III after seeing the Biedermeier furniture in the living room. Collaborating with

On the tree, bright orange clementines, a few antique ornaments, and many newly crafted cornucopias hang from the boughs, loosely swagged with magenta ribbon (opposite). Dozens of ornamental candles in metal holders clipped to the branches resemble those used on old-world Scandinavian trees.

Snippets of pine boughs give a feathery appearance to the garland of mixed greens on the living room mantel (above). The only other decoration is a pair of wooden finials painted dark green and gold. On the Biedermeier table, a burst of anemones and a pot of forced narcissus are ornaments borrowed from nature.

Webster, Goslee, who was a floral designer, draped thick evergreen garlands on mantels, hung large leafy wreaths on walls, decked paintings with emerald green boughs, and set miniature trees in tole and raffia containers for a splendid and sumptuous show of greenery. Goslee's secret was a bountiful mixing of ten different types of greens, including boxwood, pine, and balsam.

The Christmas tree, a full spruce, could have been pictured in a nineteenth-century storybook. Webster dressed it with hand-crafted cardboard cornucopias and orange clementines dangling from ribbons. Mingled with the spicy greenery, the tangy odor of fruit wafted through the rooms. And when the greenery-decked front door swung open, the unmistakable and heady fragrances of Christmas served as an invitation for guests to join David Webster's old-fashioned holiday celebration.

*C*ornucopias overflowing with penny candies were popular with the Victorians, who hung them as tree ornaments and bestowed them as toothsome treats to guests. Dee Davis, a New York City decoupage expert, re-created authentic antique designs for Webster's tree. To basic manila cones she glued fancy papers, gilt and color-printed cutouts, and passementerie trims. Then she added satin ribbon loops to hang the paper jewels from the tree.

Ropes of pine and balsam were twined around the canopy railings and down the posts of the Early American four-poster in the master bedroom (left). The lacy bedcover, delicate as snowflakes, and the Christmas-tree–green woodwork enhance the festive mood.

A Biedermeier secretary and chair provide a quiet spot for wrapping presents and writing out gift tags (below left). Boughs of pine and balsam deck the mantel and a lush wreath of laurel leaves decorates the wall.

An abundant display of fresh ripe pears, clementines, and red and green apples, arranged in bowls and baskets, introduces color and fruity fragrance to the old keeping room (opposite). The yawning fireplace, which was part of the original eighteenth-century center chimney cottage, still has the colonial iron bracket for holding pots over the fire.

Wreathing the Season in Gold

*T*he glittering decorations of Christmas ~ gold and silver glass balls piled in a sterling bowl, red sequins on a handmade butterfly ornament hovering on a tinseled branch ~ give the holiday its most magical quality. The gleam might be subtle: a few random silver stars stenciled on a white tablecloth. Or the radiance might be dazzling: a thick, sumptuous wreath of oak leaves painted copper, bronze, and gold.

At Christmas it is possible to get away with more glitter than at any other time of the year. Los Angeles designer Suzanne Rheinstein is "not a glitzy person at all," but she does believe that "at Christmas, it's time for glitz." The ropes of evergreens she hangs around her

*E*asy-to-make presents start with gold lamé fabric wrapped around the roots of miniature evergreen trees ~ available at garden centers ~ and tied with gold cord. The ornaments, which children can help bake, are star-shaped spice cookies, glazed with white sugar icing. The delicious star spangles are hung on the tree with gold ribbon.

doorways and loops on the stairway of her home are punctuated by enormous bouquets of oak and magnolia leaves, wild weeds, and pods, all burnished to a 24-carat shine with brilliant gold paint. The branches of the family tree are weighted down with dozens of hand-blown ornaments gleaming with metallic tones of red, gold, and silver.

Having special shiny ornaments that appear during the holiday season is one way to make rooms sparkle. Some people, however, like to work with reflective surfaces that decorate their rooms throughout the year. A crown that once adorned a religious statue and a Morrocan chair gleaming with mother-of-pearl inlay are two pieces that can be seen on any day in designer Victoria Hagan's office. At Christmas, however, she maximizes their luster: She might push the chair near the Christmas tree so that light can wash over the pearlescent inlay, or she might set the crown on a table bearing white narcissus.

Mirrors can be used effectively, especially when candles are placed near them so that the reflected candlelight glimmers in the silvery mirror surface. Several metallic objects can be grouped together: silver candlesticks of various sizes and shapes; a group of mercury glass spheres and cones; an assortment of old pressed-glass goblets set among silver birch branches on a mantel. With thoughtful arrangements, simple and everyday objects can lend their shine to the splendor of the holiday.

Seedpods and berry-rich greens are strewn along a mantel (above). Designer Victoria Hagan likes the contrast between rambling nature and precious gilded accessories. In another contrast of textures, she tucked whole lemons and limes among the greens.

Paul Bott gathered silvery green eucalyptus, white leptospermum, and blue spruce into a bouquet and set them in a blue toleware urn (opposite). He banked the mantelpiece with cuttings of spruce, ivy, and eucalyptus, and placed gilded apples among the greens to lend a subtle sheen.

*R*oses are everywhere at
Christmas, for good reason:
they arrive in the midst of cold
and snow with all the lushness
of a balmy summer afternoon.
Silica gel was the secret to the
ethereal beauty of Paul Bott's
rose wreath (above). Because of
the preservative, the flowers
retained all their fragile beauty
and delicate colors. Floral
designer Ronaldo Maia dried red
roses in July to create a bouquet
and headpiece for a gilded
papier-mâché angel (opposite).

A fanciful wreath blossoming with pink Evangeline roses and white lilac captures spring's magic in frosty winter (above). Floral designer Paul Bott crafted the confection, working roses, mimosa, heather, and cyclamen into a circular frame of red dogwood branches. To keep the roses fresh, he poked them into florist's water tubes. Loosely arranged snippets of eucalyptus and a silver bow with long streamers complete the exquisite design.

*I*n designer Bunny Williams's New York living room, garden expert Carolyn Gregg created a Roman-style wreath by cutting a gap in a circular Styrofoam base and covering it with florist's sheet moss (above left). The form was then completely sheathed in individual eucalyptus leaves, each anchored with a 2-inch piece of florist's wire bent into a hairpin shape. As a soft, shiny contrast to the crisp matte texture of the leaves, Gregg added a gauzy golden bow of wired ribbon.

Red roses in full bloom, garlands of juniper, and ropes of sliced dried fruit meet in a sumptuous showing on the mantel of Williams's living room (below left). Gregg ran ropes of juniper around the mirror above the fireplace and let them puddle onto the mantelpiece. She placed pinecones among the greenery and wound the juniper around the wall sconces on each side of the mirror. As a final garnish, she swagged the mantel with a weighty garland of freeze-dried fruit.

*U*tterly gilded, glittery, and glamorous, jeweled fruit and golden poinsettia leaves epitomize holiday luxury (opposite). The faux fruit, from the 1950s, has been combined with real grapefruit, pears, oranges, and grapes in a fool-the-eye arrangement. The richly carved mantel and drapery provide an appropriate background for such an ornate still life.

A painted chair becomes a gold-on-gold tableau with shimmering treasures, including a carved golden angel and a dazzling wooden sunburst (above left). A string of burnished nuts and golden wired ribbon drapes langorously over the chair back.

The effect is elegant and the technique simple for creating leaf balls set in a garden urn (below left). With a glue gun, large Styrofoam balls were covered in overlapping layers of bay leaves. As glittery garnish, streamered bows of gold ribbon were added.

$\mathcal{T}$he snow-glazed sparkle of winter is captured in tablescapes of gold and silver treasures (opposite, clockwise from top left): Two silvery glass Christmas balls, lustrous with silver glitter, are poised on a footed serving plate of mercury glass; vases of opaline glass punctuated with gold stars and white dots gather against a backdrop of gold-printed white silk; crystalline perfume bottles, frosted with gold-embossed scallops, bees, and leaves, share space with a rhinestone-studded gold minaudiere and a platinum Christmas ball crisscrossed with gold and dotted with silver glitter; a silvery grouping includes several old mercury glass vases and a frosted glass perfume bottle lit with silver-plated embossed details.

A trio of gold-flecked glass Christmas ornaments in jewel colors is a rich contrast to the all-gold surfaces of a pair of vases, a carved cornucopia, and a dimpled cherub (right).

WIT AND SPARKLE IN MANHATTAN

A red and green Christmas was not what designer Victoria Hagan imagined for her Manhattan town house. What was dancing in her head whenever she thought about decorating the two high-ceilinged rooms that serve as her office were "the funny greens and golds of Venetian glass." Not that she has anything against the holly leaf and berry hues of an old-fashioned Christmas: "My mother does a traditional Christmas, and from the time I was little I remember helping her drape the stairs with evergreens and red ribbons," she says. But for these stylish, airy spaces, where she often entertains during the holidays, Hagan wanted something entirely different.

The decorations she chose ~ ferns, gauze-wrapped fruit, and gossamer ribbon in off-tones of chartreuse and gold ~ are inspired and unconventional choices. "I wanted the atmosphere to be relaxed, with a special quality that might capture the imagination," she says. Conjuring up the snow-covered surfaces of winter, she conceived of ornaments with matte, subtly burnished finishes and placed them in seemingly random arrangements. On the table in front of an Empire sofa, many-pointed stars of dull tin and a faded metal vase of white roses were placed around a pile of books. On a fabric-draped console she scripted a tableau with

Glittering fruit gems ornamented one of Victoria Hagan's trees (opposite). She made them by wrapping dried lemons, limes, and pomegranates with sheer wired ribbon and dressmaker trimmings. Crowning the tree is a star made from dried star fruit and fern leaves.

Rather than the customary wreath, she hung a fern tied with gauzy green ribbon (above). The delicate chain of gold beads is hung from a dried clementine and secured with golden baubles.

a gold metal candelabra and a tarnished metal crown that once belonged to a religious statue, then added another vase of white flowers and a glass compote dish spilling with sugared fruit.

Hagan ordered two Christmas trees, one for each room. On one tree, she hung her own handcrafted ornaments concocted of pieces of dried fruit wrapped in gauzy ribbon, suspended on fine strings of tiny gold beads. The other tree was dressed completely in gauze bows that Hagan finished with slightly long streamers; the effect was like fluttering birds alighting on a forest tree. The homemade decor evinces both sophisticated wit and a magical, naive quality. And when the lights are dimmed and candles are lit for a holiday party, the whole room shimmers with the white luster of snow. "I think Christmas is magical," affirms Hagan, "It brings back the fondest memories of growing up."

*S*mall topiaries constructed of cloves and dried seeds mingle with seasonal bibelots, including sculptured stars of tin and a homemade ornament fashioned of a dried lime caught up in a chartreuse ribbon (below left).

Tiny candles, twinkling like fairy lights, flicker in the zany metal sconces by R. W. Russel that seem to fly above the sofa (right). Shining over the room is the glitter of a thousand glass beads in the ten-pointed star, an antique piece that comes into its own during the holidays.

*U*nexpected and simple" is the way Hagan describes her approach to holiday
decor. Resting on a damask high-back chair in her design studio is a mysterious
box tied with filmy ribbon that lends the scene a note of delicious anticipation.

At Christmas plaster wings dominate a decidedly offbeat, witty, and totally unpredictable wall tableau in Hagan's Manhattan office. Keeping them company are a gold pocket watch and bas relief visage.

A Glittering Family Holiday

Dressing the whole house in splendor is a family tradition New Orleans–born designer Suzanne Rheinstein brought with her when she moved to Los Angeles. In the South, where backyards yield enormous magnolia leaves and perfect pinecones, there is a legacy of gathering nature's bounty straight from the yard to trim the house for Christmas. Having learned early on that gold paint works a Fabergé-like transformation on an ordinary leaf, Rheinstein is a believer in handpicking seasonal decor.

Though southern California is a world away from her Louisiana roots, Rheinstein still manages to create unique and personal decorations for her Georgian Revival house. Thick ropes of mixed evergreens tumble down the sides of doorways, caught back by bouquets of gold-painted magnolia leaves. Swags are looped

There is a baroque grandeur to the evergreen garlands outlining the doorways of the Rheinstein home. The silky red streamers and gold-painted leaves underscore the refined character of the Georgian Revival house, which is filled with elegant antiques such as the Empire fainting couch seen through the doorway.

over the stair banister and the railing of the second-floor landing. Boughs rise like plumes at the tops of paintings, and gold-sprayed oak leaves crown the breakfront in the dining room. Before she had curtains, Rheinstein admits, she even honored the nineteenth-century custom of swagging the windows with lush ropes of greenery.

Rheinstein and Peter Dennis, a Los Angeles floral designer, always work out a game plan in advance, making decisions about greenery design and placement. The red silk streamers wound around the greenery are a new flourish added a couple of years ago after Rheinstein discovered a company with a process for fabricating ribbon into Fortuny-style pleats. The ribbon adds both brilliant color and texture to the evergreens, while its silky lightness allows the streamers to flutter in a beguiling manner.

The crowning glory of Rheinstein's decorating is the Christmas tree that every year sparkles with the hundreds of handblown European glass ornaments she has collected for years: a mermaid with a glittering green tail and a lady with a fluffy pink headdress of real swansdown are some of the unique members of the assemblage. Then come the strings of shiny glass beads swagged on all the branches.

With the decorating in place, the rooms become a glistening backdrop for the family's holiday entertaining. This season shared with good friends, in rooms ceremoniously dressed with evergreens, is always, says Rheinstein "a special and wonderful time."

A rope of lush greenery outlines the columns and pedimented entrance of the Rheinstein house. Magnolia leaves and seedpods, sprayed gleaming gold, dress up the wreath on the front door (above).

A wealth of handblown ornaments and swags of glass beads grace the family tree (opposite). At the very top: a German-made wax angel in a gown of pleated gold foil and gilded lace.

$\mathcal{F}$ive different types of ever-greens, including spruce and pine, are combined in the fluffy roping of greenery that tumbles over the stair rails (above). "Long, fuzzy, green pipe cleaners" are Rheinstein's secret weapon for attaching the roping to the stairway.

The breakfront wears a woodland crown of magnolia and oak leaves sprayed gold (right). Loops of red silk ribbon add a flutter of merry color. Family antiques ~ ruby-red cut-glass goblets and gold-rimmed soup bowls ~ lend their glowing patina to the dining room table.

CELEBRATING

For those who are truly fortunate, family and tradition are intertwined in the celebration of the season. Fashion designer Tommy Hilfiger had wonderful memories of his childhood Christmases in upstate New York. Now that he and his wife, Susie, have a young family of their own, new traditions are being forged. While everyone contributes to decorating the giant family tree, the couple's small children are encouraged to set up trees of their own and arrange their toys as decorations in their rooms.

Interior designer Tom Callaway is also sharing new family traditions with his wife, Claire, and young son. When the Callaways moved to Los Angeles from New York, they fell under the spell of California's Spanish colonial heritage.

Their celebration of Christmas is a spiritual one, marked by dozens of flickering lights casting a glow on the nativity scenes and religious relics the Callaways display throughout the house.

In St. Louis, decorator Suzy Grote and her husband, Richard, set up their tree in the same special spot in the foyer each year, and always have it in place by the first week in December. Visitors who fill their house each holiday delight in the tree, pictured on page 64, laden with folk ornaments the Grotes have gathered on their worldwide travels.

Many of us have our own personal rituals that put us in touch with the spirit of Christmas. For one woman, the arrival of the holiday means setting up her baking equipment on the big old pine worktable in the middle of the room and spending several days turning molasses dough into cookies shaped like reindeer, snowmen, and Santa Clauses. She began the tradition when her two daughters were small; now grown, her children still reserve a weekend before Christmas to help decorate and pack up the cookie gifts.

A winter garden all in white shimmers and sparkles with holiday joy
(opposite). A trio of fat evergreens is dressed in equally chubby gold stars
and yards of star garlands. At the table is a serious holiday workshop
where the personalized Christmas cards and the little trees with frosted
spice cookies are assembled, with gold cords gathering circles of lamé
to cover the pots (above).

THE TREE: ENDURING SYMBOL OF THE SEASON

O h, Christmas tree, Oh, Christmas tree," intones the old German carol. It is a thrilling moment when the tree is set up, for it is the centerpiece of the home Christmas celebration. Memories are rekindled as the boxes of ornaments are brought out and opened ~ here is the lacy cutout snowflake carefully scissored by a child now grown; there is the angel with the tinsel halo, today slightly faded but no less lovely, purchased on the family's first holiday together many years before. Dozens of handblown colored balls with vestiges of sprayed-on snow from Christmases past mingle with ornaments collected during a lifetime of traveling: the tiny teddy bear from England, the glass bauble striped like ribbon candy found in Italy. Soon, many ceremonies will be repeated around the tree ~ an evening devoted to tree-trimming, the placing of gifts under its branches for safekeeping, hiding a "secret" present within its boughs, and exchanging those presents on Christmas morning.

The tree blossoming with decorations was probably inspired by one of the most charming legends of Christmas: On the night of Christ's birth, goes the tale, all the trees in the forest bloomed and bore fruit. First told in the tenth century by an Arabian scholar, the tale spread over Europe and may have led to

T he beachcomber's horde of scallop shells ornamenting this tree is actually many strings of shell-shaped lights; a handmade elfin figure gazes down from the top. Designer Bill Blass chose the lights for the tree in his country home in Connecticut, proving how effective a single-theme decor can be.

the custom of bringing boughs of hawthorn and cherry trees indoors and forcing them into bloom in time for the nativity celebration. The Germans enthusiastically took over the idea, transforming the naturally blooming boughs into the artificially decorated tree. By the 1600s, fir trees began appearing in parlors at Christmas, hung with colorful paper roses, gold foil, apples, wafers, and sweets. After Prince Albert, Queen Victoria's German-born consort, decorated a tree at Windsor Castle in the 1840s, the Christmas tree ~ "that pretty German toy," Charles Dickens called it ~ became a permanent part of English and American holiday celebrations.

Today's Christmas tree can be dressed in so many ways. Some like to hang a diverse assortment of ornaments, glass balls, jolly Santa Claus figures, felt mice, and yards of colored lights, all collected over the years. Others prefer to restrict their decorations to a particular theme, embellishing the tree with only white paper doves, shiny foil fans, or beach-gathered shells; these trees are especially elegant and sophisticated even when the ornaments are simple paper cutouts. The purists may forego any adornment at all. To them, the sweet spicy scent of the pine boughs and their velvety green beauty are ornament enough. However we choose to decorate it, the Christmas tree is a wonder and delight that we look forward to every Yuletide season with childlike anticipation.

Beside a snowy barn, a handsome evergreen has been decorated just for the birds (above). Fresh oranges were scooped out and the shells filled with birdseed.

Dried grapefruit slices sparkle on a tree in East Hampton, New York (opposite). When dried, yellow grapefruit has a soft, pale color, while pink and red grapefruits are more jewel-like. To accompany the fruit are cookies made by baker Patti Paige.

*I*nterior designer Robert K. Lewis and his wife, Joy, suit their Christmas tree decorations to their house, an 1830 cottage, by dressing the boughs with Victorian-style ornaments (above). Colorful harlequins, Santa Clauses, and a honeycomb paper bell crowd on branches swagged with garlands of cranberries. Looking on from a perch on the mantel are round-bellied figures of Saint Nick.

Large double bows fashioned from wired gold and apricot ribbon were tied to the branches of a tree that Victoria Hagan set up in her design office (right). With all the boughs tied in shimmering ribbons, the plump little Douglas fir tree looked elegant, festive, and "very subtle," says Hagan.

It takes a tree at least 12 feet tall to show off all the ornaments Gary Hutton started collecting over a decade ago (opposite). The silver, gold, and crystal theme "just happened," explains the San Francisco interior designer. "About 12 years ago I came across these gigantic silver and glass ornaments that were the size of basketballs and I bought as many as I could." Since gold and silver looked wonderful with the enormous glass globes, Hutton began collecting silver stars, platinum fleurs de lis, and golden pears (left), as well as crystal icicles. The tree is a shimmering spectacle beautifully suited to the modernist surroundings of the designer's apartment in a converted industrial building.

*P*urple ribbon matches a spray of violets painted on a little teapot dangling from designer Suzanne Rheinstein's Christmas tree (left).

Christmas decorations picked from fields and woods lend shape, color, and natural beauty to this tree (below left). An abandoned birds' nest cradles eggs that were blown and then gilded to a Fabergé luster.

A rose-colored glass ball (opposite) encircled with delicate strands of pearls, a silvery tin angel, a crystalline snowflake, and a garland of blush sweetheart roses are part of the trove of glittering ornaments that one family has collected over decades. Each year they set aside four days to dress a 16-foot tree.

*B*abar the elephant and a cavorting angel are some of the beautifully made cookies on a feathery fir tree (opposite). Designed by baker Patti Paige, the cookies are decorated with vibrant-colored icing.

Nature is a limitless source of Christmas ornaments: Thistles, yarrow, ram's horns, spiral tops, lotus pods, and cane fruit are sprayed gold and become transformed into lusty sculptures (left). The delicate wreaths of reindeer moss are wrapped in slender grosgrain ribbon.

Cookies in the shape of woolly sheep gambol on writer Dee Hardie's kitchen tree (below left). Slits are cut in them before they are baked. When the cookies cool, ribbons or wire can be inserted through the holes to hang them on the tree.

A CANDLELIT CELEBRATION

*T*he spiritual aura of Christmas comes alive in Tom and Claire Callaway's family celebration in Los Angeles. Many of their most cherished treasures are religious artifacts dating from California's Catholic missionary past. At Christmas these antiques take on a heightened significance. Crucifixes hang on the kiva in the master bedroom; nativity scenes are brought out and arranged on tabletops. In the living room, the doors are gently opened on a seventeenth-century santo case, a religious piece made for private devotions. Gilded candlelabra that originally graced a Mexican church send their flickering candlelight up the enormous tree. Gazing serenely from the top branch is the carved figure of a saint wearing a golden halo. The room is hushed and peaceful as light blazes from dozens of candles.

All this has become a new family tradition. Before the move from the East Coast to California, the Callaways had always celebrated the season with quite traditional English-style decorations: rooms swagged with boughs of greenery and a tree sparkling with the sort of glass balls and baubles that are just right for a merry Dickensian Christmas. But the couple were enchanted with California's Spanish colonial heritage ~ they became intrigued with Spanish santos carvings and wooden crèche figures ~ and decided to enrich their holiday decor with its flavor.

*T*he Callaways' highly eclectic Christmas tree features their collection of Spanish and Anglo ornaments (opposite). Even the fireplace screen is decorated with a blizzard of snowflakes. In the master bedroom's kiva ~ the traditional Southwest-style fireplace ~ the main Christmas decoration is a group of antique crucifixes and small religious paintings (above). Instead of bright red Christmas stockings are simple white stockings tied with plaid ribbons.

Introducing Spanish colonial elements was appropriate for their house, built in the Mediterranean style that the Spanish colonists transported to California. The house, with stucco walls, tile floors, and hefty beams, has a hand-hewn feel, and is detailed with wrought-iron strap hinges on doors and chamfered posts, which line the gallery opening to the inner courtyard and swimming pool. Mexican wrought-iron accessories were blended into rooms with damask-covered club chairs; primitive furniture with flaking paint was set down steps away from polished mahogany. So it seemed only natural, as the couple began to decorate their Christmas tree, to make the religious antiques and artifacts a part of their celebration. Their most exciting idea was to light hundreds of candles throughout the house. Inspired by the Mexican custom of setting luminarias along outdoor walkways, Tom, a furniture and interior designer, decided to illuminate the courtyard and pool with small candle-like electric lights. Then he set real candles into dozens of votive holders and Mexican tin lanterns in the courtyard's gallery. Indoors, he placed candles in wrought-iron candelabras and added some electrified fixtures with fairy bulbs. When all are lit, the flickering beeswax candles and twinkling electric candles cast a golden glow and make the whole house radiant with burnished light. The Callaways love the theatrical drama of the blazing candlelight. "To me," says Tom, "the warmth of candlelight just says Christmas."

*I*n a modernized version of a Mexican tradition, electric lights set along the terra-cotta roof tiles and lining the pool turn the Callaways' Los Angeles courtyard into a spectacle of light at Christmastime. Lending their fire to the light show are candles set into various candelabras on tables and benches around the outdoor loggia, creating a mood both inviting and mysterious.

One of the new traditions at the Callaways: the hanging of a willow wreath on the weathered front door (left). The willow's spidery stems offer a good counterpoint to the lush potted plants that line the porch.

A vintage wooden plant stand becomes a candlelit backdrop for a display of terra-cotta crèche figures (below left). Mexican tin lanterns are arranged all around the stand, suspended from wrought-iron hooks, and positioned on wooden brackets built into the stand. When the candles are lit, the scene resembles the old Spanish missions that inspired the Callaways' decorating.

$\mathcal{E}$uropean and Pan-American traditions meet atop a sideboard showing off a miniature village scene. Little Victorian figures and tiny candle-decked Christmas trees are surrounded by small stucco Spanish-style buildings with tile roofs and arched windows. The dramatic background is a Mexican oil painting.

GIFT-GIVING AND OTHER THOUGHTFUL GESTURES

*E*xchanging presents is one of the most delightful aspects of the Christmas celebration. Part of the pleasure of gift-giving is seeking out just the right item that reflects the recipient's personality and passions: the book of Audubon watercolors for the bird lover, the brass bibelot for the antiquarian, symphony tickets for the music enthusiast. The time and thought we put into choosing presents is a way of expressing appreciation for the people we love.

The hand-made present is always eagerly received. Homemade cookies packed into a decorative tin box or a beautifully labeled jar of luscious jam tied with a fat bow are delicious treats, and the cook's care and effort never goes unappreciated. Neither does the artistry of the gifted craftsperson ~ who wouldn't love to open up the wrapping to discover a hand-knitted sweater, or bright red gloves appliquéd with polka dots? Great skill is not always even necessary to create a homemade touch. Beautiful scraps of floral chintz can be filled with potpourri and tied with soft, satin-back velvet ribbons. Inexpensive cotton placemats can be stenciled with suns and moons using silver fabric paint. These small and thoughtful gestures lift a gift out of the commercial realm and imbue it with a warm personal meaning.

*A*t the start of the holiday season, a New York couple fete friends with home-baked shortbread cookies and a puffy currant loaf (opposite). Cellophane wrap, tied with colorful ribbon, shows off the treats in all their glory. Architect William McDonough likes to hide breakable gifts in a bed of green moss, which he packs into berry boxes and ties with strands of natural raffia (above).

Creating the wrappings can fun, too. Paper embellished with stencils, gift tags of cutout snowflakes, fabric swatches transformed into wrap are among the possibilities. A striking presentation turns a trifle into a treasure. Years ago, when red and green wrapping papers were the standard, the legendary decorator Ruby Ross Wood gave her boss a little box wrapped in silver paper, bound with silver ribbon and decorated with a cluster of silver balls. He was so taken with its originality that he kept it, unopened, on his desk. He considered the fantasy of the wrapping a perfect gift in itself.

*T*he gift of spring is especially welcome at Christmas. It might take the form of a pot of fragrant forced narcissus, or, more promising still, a bag of bulbs tied with snappy tartan ribbons.

*G*ingerbread housing to delight: New York pastry chef Constance Baldwin likes to invite children in for a decorating party. Before her guests arrive, she prepares the gable-roofed gingerbread cottages (left). Royal icing serves as a sugary mortar, and candies and cookies are the architectural embellishments (above). Designs are absolutely spontaneous and no two are identical.

*I*nspired gift wraps from artists and designers would rival any gift within (clockwise from top left): Designer Brett Landenberger jazzes up plain white paper with a variety of witty ribbons; Linda Ridings-Rubino knots a hobo bag of gold-stenciled upholstery velvet; copper shines when Victoria Hagan glues on pennies, and Clodagh uses copper wire as ribbon; William McDonough gets down to basics with a plain brown paper bag, raffia, and seashells.

Sometimes the wrapping is the gift itself: packets of seeds, homemade candies, or a supply of notecards can be slipped into a beautiful terra-cotta pot (right). A mighty bow of pastel plaid ribbon and a hand-lettered gift card complete the gift.

I wanted the look of a hand-crafted package," says designer Victoria Hagan of her extravagant wrap-ups. Working with papers from an artist's supply store, she double-wrapped some presents, first with an opaque paper and then with a transparent sheet. Other gifts were wrapped in luxurious fabrics. To some boxes she attached festoons of dried leaves; others were dressed with trimmings and extra-wide ribbons from a fancy notions shop (opposite).

Angele Parlange turned a presentation box into a glittering treasure (right). The New Orleans fabric designer especially likes to work with lustrous silks. She chose coppery silk organza for this little pointed-top box and dangled jeweled baubles from its serrated edges.

HANDING ON A CHILDHOOD LEGACY

At the home of sportswear designer Tommy Hilfiger and his wife, Susie, Christmas is celebrated in virtually every room. The couple's turn-of-the-century town house in Manhattan is the ideal setting for the elaborate decorations they love. The 16-foot-high living room can easily accommodate a tree of great size; there is a bounty of mantels to dress with greens; and a winding stairway begs to be festooned with garlands. Not to be forgotten are the storybook decorations in the children's rooms. Susie Hilfiger helps their daughter, Alexandria, and son, Richard, arrange favorite toys among the garlands of pine and laurel adorning the mantelpieces in their rooms. Brightly painted wooden *Nutcracker* figures stand guard on the tiled hearth of the nursery fireplace, and a large teddy

*T*winkling with tiny lights, the Hilfigers' living room tree is always surrounded with child-size Victorian chairs (opposite). Ready to receive holiday guests with salutations is a periwigged footman with a painted vest. Plates of butter cookies are set out on tartan-covered footstools (left).

bear dressed in a scarlet Beefeater jacket is perched on the mantelpiece. Each child also has a personal tree. For her room, Alexandria asked for a tree decorated with many angels. Her mother helped her find the array of angelic ornaments: tulle-skirted angels, angels with downy feather wings, and angels with sparkling tinsel halos.

The whole family gets into the act when it comes to putting up the enormous family tree in the living room, a true Christmas setting, with red-painted walls and chintz upholstery in the red and white colors of candy canes. Everyone helps hang the old-fashioned ornaments Hilfiger has collected for years. But every Christmas, the tree's decor also gets something new. One year, family members contributed favorite personal objects as ornaments: Tommy hung up his silver baby cup and Alexandria tied on her colored hair ribbon.

Hilfiger's imaginative touches include the periwigged footmen on duty at the living room's threshold. He had them custom-made, complete with painted vests of berry red and their white powdered wigs. The Christmas stockings are Susie Hilfiger's domain. She chose traditional ones with nostalgic needlepoint designs of jolly Saint Nick to hang on the living room fireplace.

On Christmas morning, the stockings bulging with small toys and treats are the first gifts the children rush for. Then everyone kneels around the tree to exchange presents. "I have always loved an old-fashioned, traditional Christmas at home with my family," says Hilfiger.

*W*earing festive ribbons, old-fashioned teddy bears await the holiday on a plaid-covered bench in the foyer.

$\mathcal{T}$he ruddy tones of apples and pears lend cheer to the pine rope on the living room mantel. The lush greenery is placed so that it spills over each end, creating a look of rich abundance. Standing guard are a pair of pert Staffordshire dogs, each wearing a festive plaid neck bow.

Turning Back the Christmas Clock

Wonderful examples of Christmas decorations go on view at historic houses throughout America during the holidays. These grand showings are public celebrations of our national Christmas heritage. At Colonial Williamsburg, Virginia, fruit-rich topiaries and wreaths dress sideboards and tables. Historic Charleston, South Carolina, hosts tours of its fine old homes, festooned inside and out with artfully arranged wreaths, garlands, and greenery. In Jackson, Mississippi, the nineteenth-century Manship House offers candlelight tours. The results of months of careful planning, the exquisite displays that these historic houses sponsor are a rich source of Christmas decorating inspiration.

Christmas comes early at Chesterwood in Stockbridge, Massachusetts, in the heart of the Berkshire Mountains. The house is decked for the holidays and open to visitors in mid-November as part of a community fund-raising project. In the first decades of this century, Chesterwood was the much-loved home of Daniel Chester French, the famous American sculptor whose bronze minuteman presides over the grassy park in Concord, where the first shots of the Revolutionary War were fired.

"We try to decorate the house in the style that would be appropriate to 1910 or 1920," says curator Linda Jackson, who helps administer

The bosky wallpaper Daniel Chester French brought back from Europe forms a rich background for Christmas celebrations decades later (opposite). Evergreens cascading over the banister are punctuated by nosegays of dried roses cradled in lace doilies and caught up with pink ribbon streamers.

Antique serving pieces and ripe natural fruit combine in the dining room's dramatic decor (above). The table centerpiece is an elaborate epergne of crystal and silver, surrounded by sprays of greenery and fruit.

Chesterwood, which is now a property of the National Trust for Historic Preservation. Each year she and director Paul Ivory choose a different design theme and invite members of the community to join in the decorating activity. Area garden clubs, florists, decorators, and antiques shops participate. These experts often lend their own collections of period accessories and antique toys, mixing them with furniture and china that French's family purchased on their many trips to Italy and France. No matter what the theme, the thousands of visitors who come for Christmas at Chesterwood are assured of sharing in a heartwarming holiday that is truly old-fashioned in spirit.

*L*aid out for a holiday tea, the table in the reception room of the sculpture studio sparkles with fine china and silver servers filled with Christmas cookies (above right). Pink ribbons on the branches of the tree match the flowing skirt; the lacy tea cloth over it is an exquisite example of skilled embroidery and cutwork.

Upstairs, one bedroom looks as though it was decorated especially for the holiday (right). As a child, Margaret French Cresson, the daughter of Daniel French, would awaken to Christmas morning under the gauzy canopy of her four-poster bed.

A magic toyland is arranged around the Christmas tree in the parlor. A doll with golden curls and a large dollhouse with its own miniature Christmas trees evoke the turn-of-the-century era when Chesterwood was built. Period ornaments, including paper angels and snowflakes, are carefully hung on the tree, together with snowy ropes of popcorn.

ENTERTAINING

Without the parties, dinners, and festive seasonal galas, Christmas simply would not be Christmas. Guest lists are drawn up and invitations mailed for open houses that welcome a grand crowd of friends and acquaintances. Gilt-edged cards bearing exquisite calligraphy may also go out beckoning close friends to a more intimate party, perhaps a fireside supper like the one Richard Lowell Neas planned when he decorated a dining room with beautifully bare trees, pictured on the opposite page.

On each of these occasions the creative presentation of food enhances the welcome we extend. In many families a particular recipe presented in a special way is an annual family tradition. Suzanne Rheinstein's Christmas Eve

dinner always starts with wild mushroom consommé flavored with dollops of salty whipped cream, set forth in gold-rimmed soup bowls that once belonged to her mother.

Family tradition also governs John Saladino's offerings at Christmas: smoked salmon on tree-shaped pieces of toast, served on a table spectacularly dressed with his collections of antiques. Other designers also polish up their collectibles to use as holiday serving pieces. Tulsa decorator Charles Faudrée presses

his collection of Victorian silver christening mugs into service as eggnog cups. Tom Pritchard takes special pleasure in finding new roles for many of his utilitarian antiques: Freshly shucked oysters are served on ice in an old treenware bowl, and vintage round bread boards are converted into handy, one-of-a-kind platters. And when Pritchard needs a tray to present cheeses and breads to his guests, he reaches for a huge wooden slab a farmer once used for winnowing grain.

A SERVING OF TABLE MAGIC

Sitting down at a table with a group of people is one of the most rewarding experiences," says Atlanta chef and food consultant Scott Peacock, "and especially so during the holidays." Whether it is a luncheon for eight or a champagne supper for twenty, a holiday meal always seems to have the exciting feeling of ceremony attached to it. To underscore this sense of celebration, imaginative table settings are definitely in order. Some hosts and hostesses relish Christmas dinners as a time to create the most luxurious table decorations. Silver place plates and antique covered entrée dishes gleam on a tablecloth made of red Indian silk when Marjorie Reed Gordon, an author of books on entertaining, and her husband, Ellery, throw their annual Christmas dinner. For many hosts, long guest lists do not daunt their tabletop extravagance: Fine damask and linen napkins do not really need matching monograms, provided they all share a snowy whiteness. Set side-by-side with silver chargers, silver candlesticks, and silver accessories, the effect is pure magic.

But others prefer the simple decorations of nature for their holiday tables. Designer Richard Lowell Neas likes to arrange ribbons of real ivy on a plain white cloth with a natural centerpiece of spring bulbs. His tableware is also simple: elegant white porcelain with discreet embossed motifs in blue, as well as plain wine

The holiday table provides a reason to bring out the most prized table linens. For one homeowner, the cloth is an old-world treasure, a lace-encrusted tea cloth that traditionally marks the holiday on a round table (opposite). Lyre-backed chairs add their own grace note to the intimate setting.

glasses in pleasing round and tulip shapes. "Good food shared with good friends doesn't really need a lot of decoration," says Neas.

Although a seated dinner can mean more work, keeping things simple will save time and nerves, maintains Peri Wolfman, co-owner of a Manhattan tablewares shop. Her guidelines: a basic color scheme such as white and green and a flat of flowers as an instant centerpiece. When it comes to planning the menu, simplicity is also Scott Peacock's watchword. Choose dishes that are not complicated and try to make a couple of them ahead of time, he advises: "Nothing should keep you away from the table more than five minutes."

*T*he flowers of spring ~ lilies of the valley, narcissus, and tulips ~ are the natural decorations that designer Richard Lowell Neas chose for a Christmas luncheon. The green and white blossoming bulbs inspired the palette for the table setting: On the heavy white matelassé cloth he laid cuttings of rich green ivy. The lilies of the valley bursting forth from the blue-and-white porcelain centerpiece fill the room with fragrance; for the designer's luncheon guests, it is a sweet, and unexpected, note of spring in December.

*F*resh green herbs can be an
alternative to pine and poinsettias
for a holiday table (opposite).
The tiny Christmas tree gracing
each place setting was made
from fresh-cut rosemary
arranged in a florist's oasis that
had been placed in a small clay
pot. As a glittery ornament,
gold ribbon was swagged loosely
around each one, but tiny
glass balls or other miniature
decorations would also be lovely.

Crystal and silver sparkle
against a cyclamen-colored
tablecloth at a dinner given by
writer Marjorie Reed Gordon
(right). The table is set with
silver serving plates and fluted
silver vases filled with fresh-
cut white amaryllis flowers.
Gordon's personal touch at
each place setting: a silver
beaker cradling a pomander ~
lovely favors for each guest
to take home.

For her family's Christmas dinner, Connecticut designer Sandy Ceppos likes to depart from the predictable: instead of red or white, she prefers table linens in teal, a color choice that adds zest to the antique wood table and pumpkin-hued dining room. Ceppos's holiday decor also gives tradition a twist. Whole dried hydrangeas bloom on the mantel, and small bouquets of dried flowers blossom on the tree.

THEATER OF THE FANTASTIC

I love the theater of Christmas, the fantasy of this brief time when we can address childlike things again," says John Saladino. The Manhattan designer always spends Christmas entertaining houseguests at his country retreat. And every other year or so, he indulges his taste for theatrical fantasy by hosting a splendid party the week before Christmas. For the black-tie gala, his houseguests are joined by friends from Manhattan and some of Saladino's neighbors in the Connecticut Berkshires.

The planning begins a full two months before the party. Orders are placed for invitations engraved on fine English paper, along with RSVP cards and envelopes on which each guest's name is written in flowing calligraphy. A color theme for the decorations is selected: One year it may be silver, another it is burgundy and gold. Marshaling the expertise and energy of his office staff, Saladino reviews every detail. Containers for favors are considered, fabrics for tablecloths are pondered, and the menu is carefully planned.

For one grand Christmas, the silver tones of platinum and sterling glistened throughout Saladino's house. The most extravagant display was reserved for the two dining rooms: Saladino turned them into wondrous ice-palace interiors. Against walls painted a pale tint of periwinkle,

E very room at John Saladino's Connecticut house is garbed for entertaining. In the grand drawing room, the massive Christmas tree wears its customary raiment of treasured family ornaments.

the designer dressed the dining tables in silver Mylar, creating metallic skirts that flowed to the floor. At each place setting he positioned an ice-white plate atop a silver charger. Other pieces from his collection of antique silver were carefully set on the table: handsome candlesticks, small shell-shaped dishes, and fine flatware. To create the illusion of a snowy forest, bare, silvery tree branches were placed on the tables amid tapering white candles. When the candles were lit, the rooms became wonderlands of enchantment, bringing to life the theatrical magic John Saladino loves to create at Christmastime.

At Christmas, virtually every room in John Saladino's house is decorated with bounty gathered from the surrounding woodland. Rosy-cheeked lady apples are cradled in a basket of rustic twigs (left). A red napkin tucked under the fruit bestows a stroke of festive color.

In the intimate sitting room (opposite), two huge bunches of fir boughs held by verdigris metal bow knots grace the paneled hearth; the wreath is fashioned of twigs and birds' feathers.

*T*he dining room resembles a magic grove of silver birches (left). Lending their sterling gleam to the silvery decor are several antique serving pieces arranged on the sideboard.

All in frosty colors of white and silver, the table is set with an inspired combination of formal and informal elements (above). There are four patterns of elegant silver flatware, a different design for each course. Casual touches include pearly ribbon streamers tied around napkins and garlands of tiny glass beads looped like necklaces on the tabletop.

THE PLEASURE OF THEIR COMPANY

*T*he holiday season presents many imaginative possibilities for gatherings, and perhaps none is as versatile or enjoyable as the buffet. The occasion might be as informal as the breakfast buffet at Tom Pritchard's Catskill Mountain retreat. When his clan wakes up Christmas morning, they head for the kitchen, where Pritchard arranges on the hearth-front table delicious jams and plump English muffins he bakes in the wood stove. Or the buffet might be an open house, like the one designer Robert K. Lewis and his wife, Joy, host every Christmas Eve at their historic Long Island house. Savory dishes such as ham and smoked turkey are displayed on one table; another offers up footed plates of sweets and fruit. Intriguing small antiques ~ an architectural model of a house, a German candy container shaped like a rabbit ~ are poised on tables among pots of flowering narcissus.

Still another excuse for a buffet is provided by the toothsome desserts of the season. On Christmas evening San Francisco designer Gary Hutton always invites about 20 friends to enjoy coffee and luscious confections arranged on a table in front of his 12-foot-high tree, shimmering with gold and silver ornaments.

A buffet might also accompany a caroling party, a tree-trimming with family and friends, or a children's afternoon of baking and icing

A carpet of emerald-green leaves laid on the sideboard and an ethereal landscape painting give an assemblage of spectacular desserts a fantasy stage set. Any one of these would also be a decorative grand finale in its own right: a bûche de Noël wrapped in chocolate bark, a croquembouche constructed of cream puffs with clouds of spun sugar, and a chocolate-glazed orange cake ringed with kumquats.

sugar cookies. Because buffets are by definition more casual than sit-down meals, any room can be adapted to serving and seating. A buffet party might even be planned as a moveable feast, with successive courses served in different parts of the house: a warming soup in the entrance hall, the main course in the dining room, and dessert by the fire in the living room.

From a practical point of view, a buffet offers ease for the host or hostess, who will welcome convenience at this busy time of year. Many dishes can be prepared ahead of time and frozen. Since guests serve themselves, there is no need to worry about circulating hors d'oeuvres or serving at table. Guests also reap their own benefits from a buffet party ~ they get to mingle more and can eat just what they want.

*L*ike many of the best hosts, Tom Pritchard maximizes the impact and minimizes the effort when he entertains (left). Buffets are his solution. On a table dressed with flowers and antique candlesticks, he serves a delicious holiday dinner: exotic cheeses, chilled oysters, and champagne with homemade soup and chewy bread.

Pritchard's serving style and menu for Christmas breakfast are more casual than the one for Christmas Eve, but no less tempting (right). He arranges, so guests can choose and prepare for themselves, jars of homemade jams and English muffins, jumbo brown eggs, oranges, and earthenware teapots filled with steaming Earl Grey.

*T*hink of color and texture as well as flavor if you want a buffet to have a festive air," says chef and caterer Carole Peck, who planned a party in a colonial New England setting. Her choices ~ bright red tomato slices with green snap peas, dollops of red and black caviar on crab cakes ~ demonstrate her philosophy. Brass candlesticks in a variety of tubular and spiral shapes are enough decoration for this colorful feast.

*T*win Christmas trees glistening with icicles, silver balls, and candles stand guard
on a hearthside buffet. The rich culinary traditions of Christmas in the South
inspired the array of dishes: ham biscuits, pear and apple ambrosia, cornmeal
buns and, on an ornate sterling serving dish, a golden fruitcake ~ all cooked up
by talented southern-born food expert Sarah Belk. To toast the day, champagne
chills in an ice-filled antique porcelain jardinière.

*T*wo dessert buffets were orchestrated by Carole Peck. A selection ranging
from tart to very sweet includes chèvre tart and a fig and cherry cake with
lemon curd (above). The red paisley table skirt provides a colorful,
sophisticated stage. On another table, this one set with unmatched patterns
of blue-and-white china ~ English Staffordshire dessert plates and Canton
teacups and saucers ~ a bittersweet chocolate terrine and a crystallized
ginger walnut torte stand ready (opposite). Full-blown red tulips bloom
in a blue-and-white Delft-style footed cachepot.

With sugary treats on footed stands and tiered servers, the tea that Manhattan designer Dennis Rolland holds for a Sunday afternoon open house is a picture of Edwardian elegance. A menu of finger-food delicacies like these, made in advance, overcomes the cooking and serving restraints of a small kitchen.

A fireside butler's tray is the elegant serving station for sherry at the
New York City design shop of Charlotte Moss. To give a cheerful air to
the mantel, floral designer Paul Bott posed apples, pears, and grapes among
antique porcelains, along with fresh mimosa branches and sprays of pine.

A TWO-PARTY AFFAIR

Tulsa decorator Charles Faudrée and his sister, Francie Faudrée, celebrate Christmas with two traditional parties everyone they know looks forward to. Shortly after Thanksgiving, over one hundred invitations go out to clients and friends for a formal tea, always held on a December weekend. "We always have a lot of people," says Charles Faudrée, "and it's usually from 2 to 4, or 4 to 6 in the evening." Along with steaming tea and delicious, tempting cakes, there is usually a frothy bowl of eggnog. Serving that creamy Christmas drink provides Faudrée with a grand excuse to bring out his collection of sterling and silverplate antique christening mugs to pass around to guests. At last count there were over fifty mugs, mostly English Victorian and Edwardian. "It's the only time I get to use them," says the designer.

A more intimate celebration is the Christmas Eve supper the Faudrées jokingly call their "party for waifs and strays." The guest list runs from eight to 20, depending, says Faudrée, "on who is around and who is without a family that year." The name for the party was inspired by an old toy he found in England ~ a small drum with the name of an orphanage, Institute for Waifs and Strays, stenciled on it.

Late on Christmas Eve, snacks and champagne are served on Charles Faudrée's stone-paved porch, warmed by a roaring fire (opposite). Served with a seasonal champagne toast, homemade peach pie is one of the Faudrée family specialties (above). The rustic English table rests on a base of tree limbs; a wreath and glowing antique candelabra imbue it with Christmas spirit.

"When you don't have a large family, it's important to go somewhere on Christmas Eve," says Faudrée. Some years the party is at his house, other years at his sister's. Since the Faudrées work late on Christmas Eve at their antiques and decorating shop, they have worked out an organized plan to make the party run smoothly. An essential part of their strategy is caterer Jody Walls, who prepares a hearty meal that sometimes includes a homemade soup. The soup for all these guests is served in Faudrée's collection of magnificent blue-and-white antique tureens. "Jody doesn't mind when we keep adding to the guest list," says the designer.

One year the Faudrées also had assistance from Tom Pritchard, the New York City floral designer. Pritchard is known for his lavish displays of greenery done in extravagant yet natural-looking arrangements. He placed greenery and branches of forced blossoms to show off Faudrée's many unusual antiques and porcelains.

Most of Faudrée's furnishings are French. He travels to Paris twice a year to buy for the shop and never fails to come across something unique for his own home as well. The game plaque on the porch mantel, around which Tom Pritchard wired juniper branches, is one find that came from Paris. Such decorative treasures stay at home, confesses Charles Faudrée, "because they are so perfect for Christmas parties."

Juniper branches thick with berries were set on the kitchen counter by floral designer Tom Pritchard, who helped decorate for Charles and Francie Faudrée's Christmas Eve supper. Because the kitchen is the center of activity, Pritchard decked the room lavishly. He placed bouquets of fresh-cut red amaryllis on the counters and even tucked spruce boughs around the antique pigeonnier suspended from the ceiling.

A jardinière filled with white clouds of forced spirea blossoms is the main decoration in the sun room, where the Faudrée family opens presents on Christmas morning (above). The plates and platters grouped on walls are part of Charles Faudrée's large collection of blue-and-white English Staffordshire.

A crackling fire and the warm glow of candles invite guests into the living room for cheese and crackers (opposite). Candles are arranged to illuminate the full-blooming roses on the coffee table and holly draped around sconces over the mantel. On the fireside table the flickering reflection of a candle flame can be seen in the glass dome containing a Victorian figure of Father Christmas.

Directory of Designers

Constance Baldwin
Constance Baldwin Productions
New York, New York

Laura Bohn
Lembo Bohn Design Associates
New York, New York

Paul Bott
Paul Bott Beautiful Flowers
New York, New York

Tom Callaway
Thomas Callaway Bench Works
Los Angeles, California

Sandy Ceppos
Designs for the Home
New Canaan, Connecticut

Clodagh
Clodagh Design International
New York, New York

Bill Crinnigan
Bill Crinnigan Inc.
New York, New York

Dee Davis
Adventures in Crafts
New York, New York

Elizabeth Demetriades
Elizabeth Demetriades Architecture
Ancramdale, New York

Peter Dennis
Whitegate
Los Angeles, California

Michael Erikson
New York, New York

Charles Faudrée
Charles Faudrée Antiques & Interiors
Tulsa, Oklahoma

Jack Follmer, Jr.
VSF
New York, New York

Carolyn Gregg
Treillage
New York, New York

Victoria Hagan
Victoria Hagan Interiors
New York, New York

Allen C. Haskell
Allen Haskell Nursery
New Bedford, Massachusetts

Gary Hutton
Gary Hutton Design
San Francisco, California

Sura Kayla
Sura Kayla Floral Design
New York, New York

Brett Landenberger
San Francisco, California

Robert K. Lewis
Robert K. Lewis Associates
New York, New York

David Madison
Horticultural Design Inc.
New York, New York

Ronaldo Maia
Ronaldo Maia Ltd.
New York, New York

William McDonough
William McDonough Architects
New York, New York

Charlotte Moss
Charlotte Moss & Company
New York, New York

Richard Lowell Neas
Richard Neas Interiors
New York, New York

Patti Paige
Baked Ideas
New York, New York

Angele Parlange
New Orleans, Louisiana

Scott Peacock
The Horseradish Grill
Atlanta, Georgia

Carole Peck
Good News Café
Woodbury, Connecticut

Tom Pritchard
Pure Mädderlake
New York, New York

Christopher Radko
New York, New York

Suzanne Rheinstein
Hollyhock
Los Angeles, California

Linda Ridings-Rubino
Atlanta, Georgia

Spruce Roden
VSF
New York, New York

Dennis Rolland
Dennis Rolland Inc.
New York, New York

John Saladino
John F. Saladino Inc.
New York, New York

David Webster
New York, New York

Bunny Williams
Bunny Williams Inc.
New York, New York

Peri Wolfman
Wolfman-Gold & Good Company
New York, New York

Zezé
Zezé Flowers
New York, New York

The antique angel on page 1 is from Linn Howard; page 2, starfish ornaments designed by Nancy Gaudioso Lutz; page 4, the bird's nest by Carrie Glenn; page 7, angel and cherub by Natalie Silitch; page 8, room designed by David Webster and Michael Erikson; page 9, handblown ornament (top) by Christopher Radko; page 11, topiary by Treillage; page 12, basket by Allen C. Haskell; page 15, dried cockscomb wreath by Sura Kayla; page 140, wreath by Sura Kayla.

House Beautiful *would like to acknowledge the following homeowners: Alice and Walter McAdams, Lloyd and Leslie Allen, JoAnn and Fred Berger, John and Linda Cross, Thomas and Dee Hardie, Ellery and Margery Reed Gordon.*

PHOTOGRAPHY CREDITS

1	Thibault Jeanson	46	Lizzie Himmel	92	Catherine Leuthold
2-8	James Cooper	47	Billy Cunningham		(top and bottom right)
9	Jeremy Samuelson (top)	48	Jesse Gerstein		Antoine Bootz
	Antoine Bootz (bottom)	49	Antoine Bootz		(bottom left)
11	James Cooper	50, 51	Edward Addeo	93	Zeva Oelbaum
12	Kari Haavisto	52-57	Andrew Garn	94	Andrew Garn
15	Antoine Bootz	58-63	Jeremy Samuelson	95	Catherine Leuthold
16	Jeff McNamara	64	Karen Radkai	96-99	Antoine Bootz
17	Andrew Garn	65	Jack Winston	100-103	Lizzie Himmel
18	Lynn Karlin	66, 67	Lizzie Himmel	104	Karen Radkai
19, 20	Antoine Bootz	68	Richard Felber	105-107	Kari Haavisto
21	Michael Skott	70	Michael Skott	108	Elyse Lewin
22	Kari Haavisto	71	Kit Latham	110-111	Karen Radkai
23	Antoine Bootz	72	William P. Steele	112	Rita Maas
24	Jeremy Samuelson	72-73	Andrew Garn	113-115	Kari Haavisto
25, 26	Lizzie Himmel	74, 75	Jack Winston	116-121	David Frazier
27	Antoine Bootz	76	Jeremy Samuelson (top)	122	Marina Schinz
28	Jesse Gerstein		William P. Steele	124-125	Michael Skott
29	Fran Brennan		(bottom)	126	Langdon Clay
30	Antoine Bootz	77	Walter Smalling	127	Lizzie Himmel
31	Langdon Clay	78	Kit Latham	128, 129	Langdon Clay
32, 33	Antoine Bootz	79	Peter Bosch (top)	130	Michael Skott
34-40	Lizzie Himmel		Lilo Raymond (bottom)	131	Lizzie Himmel
42	Andrew Garn	80-85	Tim Street-Porter	132-137	Langdon Clay
43	Lizzie Himmel	86	Alex McClean	140	James Cooper
44	Marina Schinz	87	Antoine Bootz	142-143	Kari Haavisto
45	Jeff McNamara	88-89	Elizabeth Watt	144	Antoine Bootz
		90, 91	Elizabeth Zeschin